Poems From a Failing Society

Ryan Lyddall

Dedicating this book was harder than writing it. There have been so many people who have helped me over the past few years, helped me to improve the book and helped me to improve myself.

I can't name you all, but thank you to all my friends and family for your support. I would not be the person I am today without your love, and I would never have been able to write this book.

But while I have the opportunity, I have to give a special thank you to my found family at Karuna. Simon, Jessica, Louise, Aggi, Bruce and all the volunteers who support us.

I love you all, thank you for shining a light in the darkness.

Foreword | By Ash Hirst

Ryan Lyddall is a full time creative, activist and barista living and working in Aldershot, UK.

By day he works at Karuna Coffee House - a non-profit coffee shop which raises funds for Karuna Action, a poverty relief charity that does amazing work providing healthcare and education around the globe. In his spare time he is the secretary for the Aldershot branch of the Socialist Party, a revolutionary party fighting to improve the lives of working-class people, and bring about socialist change to our society.

Ryan has dedicated his life to the reduction of suffering - realised in this book through his insights on the omnipresent smothering forces of capitalism, the animal agriculture industry and many other interlinking issues facing our society.

He is frequently outspoken in his views, and anyone who is lucky enough to meet him (even for a few minutes) is guaranteed to walk away with a new friend, world view and an extensive reading list.

Whilst raising class consciousness and bringing an end to capitalism are his main goals, Ryan has many other areas of interest - and I feel it would be unjust not to mention Magic the Gathering as one of these. The reason I bring this up is because Ryan credits a video essay made by Magic YouTuber Spice8Rack *(Anarchism & Police Abolition | Feat. Domn Rade)* as the spark that ignited the anti-calitalist fire within him.

There is infinitely more I could tell you about Ryan, much more than can be contained in this brief foreword, so I should end this by actually doing my job and telling you how amazing this book is and how proud we are of him. I hope you enjoy this book as much as I have.

Introduction

"This book is not concerned with poetry... All the poet can do today is to warn, that is why true poets must be truthful."

-*Wilfred Owen*

I am no Wilfred Owen, but my approach to writing has been inspired by this quote. I understand how someone reading these poems could walk away thinking that I hate this world, but I promise you I don't. Despite all the issues I have with how our society functions, they have not robbed me of my appreciation of the beauty of our planet, or the beauty of human potential.

Writing this book has been a challenge, but it has also been a cathartic experience. The problems I tackle in this anthology are problems that hang over every day of my life, leaving me feeling powerless and overwhelmed. I understand why some choose ignorant bliss over painful reality, but it is a choice that will cost us all in the long run. Unless we do the hard work and address the structural issues of our society now, the problems will just continue to get worse. At the moment all we are doing is paying lip service to issues that, if left unaddressed, will only grow more dire.

This book deals with the demons of our society, but it also deals with some of my personal demons. I considered not including the sections on mental health and addiction, but felt that my personal experiences will hopefully allow others to feel less alone in their struggles. And ultimately, issues surrounding mental health and addiction are symptoms of the society we live in.

I hope you enjoy this anthology, and I hope it challenges how you think. Despite the depressing nature of the subject matter, the point of this book for me isn't misery, but hope.

It is never too late for a bad person to do good. The bad they have done is never forgotten and they may never be redeemed, but it is never too late for them to choose to start doing good.

In the same vein - it is never too late to change the world, it is never too late to save the world. The damage of the past is already done, but we can save what remains.

We must save what remains.

Poem For a Failing Society

The world in which we are raised
Is how we think the world must be.
We know nothing other
Than this failing society.

So many of our thoughts
Are not truly our own.
We're indoctrinated from birth
To believe what we're shown.

We're brainwashed by propaganda,
Our minds have been moulded.
We're surrounded by suffering
But they keep us blindfolded.

Our society survives
Through death and exploitation.
Hidden beneath the surface,
Not taught in our education.

We are told that this is it,
There's nothing else you see.
We must learn to accept
That this is our reality.

The holes are covered,
The cracks are hidden.
We refuse to improve
The alternative is forbidden.

We march towards our demise
Blinded by our complacency,
Unaware of our potential
To save our society.

Poems From a Failing Society

Capitalism - 1

Animal Rights - 21

Climate Change - 45

LGBT Rights - 63

Mental Health - 83

Addiction - 109

Palestine - 133

War - 153

Capitalism

Based on "The Conditions Of Labouring Man At Pullmans"
from the Chicago Labour Newspaper

Capitalism thrives while the majority of the populace do not really understand what capitalism means. If we ever want to see a post-capitalist society then one of the first steps is helping people connect their day to day struggles with the structural issues of capitalism.

Do not be fooled into believing that capitalism is human nature. It is a part of our story, the part we are currently living through, but it doesn't have to be the final chapter.

Capitalism

God and the Devil - 5

Capitalism! - 6

Cost of Convenience - 8

Artificial Scarcity - 9

Mad - 10

Media - 11

Bad Laws - 12

The System Isn't Broken - 14

If Jesus Was Alive Today - 15

Great Britain - 16

Strikes - 17

Communism! - 18

When? - 19

Capitalism | Opening Thoughts

My friends often joke that I blame capitalism for everything, but the truth is that I really do believe that it is responsible for the vast majority of problems facing our world.

As long as there is a profit to be made from destroying the planet, killing animals and selling weapons, none of these things will stop.

Capitalism is a system that disregards morality and cares only about the accumulation of wealth into the hands of a few, regardless of how many people are exploited in the process.

When people tell me we don't need to overthrow capitalism, and that we can instead fix it, it tells me that they do not truly understand what kind of beast capitalism is.

The exploitation of workers, the destruction of our planet and the furthering divide between the rich and the poor are not problems with capitalism, they are the very essence of capitalism.

Capitalist greed is unending, and it will make humanity devour itself unless we stop it.

God and the Devil

I don't believe in God
For he remains hidden,
But I've witnessed the Devil
In the hands of a politician.

His will is enacted
Through the coins man desires.
Where our blind lust for money
Converts honest men into liars.

The preachers in the church
Are clawing for money.
God's just a product,
Does he find it funny?

The old God is dead,
It's sad but it's true.
Worship money instead
God has no value.

God may once have made
Men, animals and trees,
But the Devil's in charge now
And nothing is free.

If men ever want
To know God again,
Stop worshiping money
It won't happen 'til then.

Capitalism!

Capitalism is great!
Why would you complain?
You must be stupid!
Do you have half a brain?

Haven't you heard?
Capitalism breeds innovation!
You can do anything,
With enough dedication!

Thanks to the system
We have so much choice!
It gives us all we desire
So we should all rejoice!

If you put in the work
You will all be rewarded.
Ignore all the money
We've already hoarded.

The game is just!
And the game is fair!
The game doesn't require
Someone else's despair.

So keep your head up
And play your part.
Ignore the longing
You feel in your heart.

You work all-day
And you work all-night.
If you make enough money
You might be alright.

You can do what you want
Unless you want to be free.
Freedoms an illusion,
We're all slaves to money.

Capitalism is great
If you're a billionaire.
The poor might be suffering
But we don't really care.

The Cost of Convenience

That shirt costs how much?
Those shoes were so cheap!
With all of these savings
I'll have a good nights sleep.

But the workers who made them
Will work 'til they weep,
In miserable conditions
Who cares how they sleep?

The cost is low
Yet the profit is high.
The workers are suffering
But we turn a blind eye.

The true price of the product
Is not only its cost,
But the poor foreign workers
Whose lives have been lost.

Artificial Scarcity

We have plenty of diamonds
But we'll tell you they're rare.
Buy one for your partner
Or they'll think you don't care.

We control all the markets,
We control all the supply,
We pay off the media
To cover up our lie.

Consumers are stupid!
They'll do what we say.
Just put up some billboards,
The consumers will pay.

Pay the workers poorly,
Pay the shareholders well.
Don't think about morality,
Our diamonds have to sell.

Mad

Sometimes I worry
I'm going insane.
I worry there is something
Very wrong with my brain.

I'm worried I'm crazy,
I'm worried I'm mad.
When I worry I cry
And when I cry I am sad.

I worry for the animals,
I worry for the poor.
I feel like every day
I worry more and more.

But the system is the way it is
And the way it is is the way it must.
So don't complain,
Ignore the pain,
Because the system is because the system is.

But that seems crazy
To little old me.
I think something's wrong
But the system loves to disagree.

So either I must be mad
And should be locked away,
Or the system is bad
And we've all been led astray.

Media - Co-written with Kalian Uddin Askew

The TV's your friend
From start until end.
We help you to think,
Without us you'd sink.

All you are told
And all you are shown
Is far from the truth
But it's all that you've known.

The promises and tales,
The lie never fails,
Made for you and made for me
Live right now on your TV.

We might show you the truth,
But only a glance.
Then we'll distract you
With a song and a dance.

Who are you to decide
What's worth your attention?
We'll do that for you,
Make no objection.

But please do stay,
Trust we know the way.
Clearly your ignorance is bliss,
You've become your own nemesis.

Bad Laws

Good people might
Not follow some laws
That might sound strange
But they do it because
Good people should
Break bad laws
Knowing they might never
Receive any applause

Some people think
Law equates to morality
But look to the past
And it's easy to see
The law ain't always here
For you and for me
But to protect the interests
Of the bourgeoisie

Slavery was legal
For way too long
But it being legal
Didn't make it not wrong
Some people were brave
Some people were strong
And fought the law
To hurry change along

The law's not perfect
It's been wrong in the past
We've changed it before
But change is never fast
And that change didn't happen
Because people kindly asked
They resisted and fought
And change happened at last

Blindly following the law
Can be a fatal mistake
Laws promise to protect us
But those promises are fake
Because if we don't fight back
They'll take and they'll take
To be a good person
Bad laws you should break

The System Isn't Broken

They say the system's broken.
Oh how I wish that was true.
The system isn't broken,
It just doesn't care for me or you.

This system has one purpose,
To hoard wealth for the greedy.
The system's not concerned,
With the suffering of the needy.

So who cares if you struggle?
And who cares if you die?
The system wasn't built for you -
Your needs don't apply.

If Jesus Was Alive Today

If Jesus was alive today
What would he think
And what would he say

If Jesus saw how we treat the poor
Could he in good conscience
Show us Heavens door

If Jesus saw how we treat the needy
Would he stop being Jesus
And punish the greedy

Jesus tried to teach peace
And he tried to teach love
And yet we're determined
To rain bombs from above

Jesus wouldn't care for coins
Or our western luxuries
All he would care for is the suffering
Those luxuries cost overseas

I think if Jesus saw
What we did in his name
He would turn his head
And hang it in shame

Great Britain

I don't really see
What's so great about Britain,
We should learn from the past
But ours is being hidden.

I don't feel honour
And I don't feel pride
That because of my country
So many people have died.

Our country isn't great,
Saying it is is a joke.
Our politicians are rich
But our hospitals are broke.

How can we claim
To be a great nation
When our teens are depressed
And all need medication?

How can we claim
To be a great nation
When we let our own children
Die of starvation?

Strikes

When the system is full
Of such obvious faults,
Who can blame the worker
Who finally revolts?

When the workers are mad
And the workers don't like
The greed of the bosses,
The workers will strike.

The bosses will try
To stop our protest,
They'll villainize the workers
And threaten them with arrest.

But the workers stay stong
And they keep up the fight,
Because the workers know
They fight for what's right.

Communism!

You should hate communism,
Even if you don't understand.
In fact that's better
Their books should be banned!

Communism is evil
Barbaric and cruel,
And if you support it
You're an ignorant fool.

Communism never works
Whenever it tries,
The capitalists ensure it
When they send in their spies.

But maybe take a minute
And question what you've been told
You've been fed propaganda
From the people hoarding gold

Communism is bad
If you're a billionaire
Because billionaires don't like it
When everything is fair.

When?

When I speak of revolution,
"When will it happen?" is all they say.
"This revolutionary movement
Seems so far away."

"Why should we waste our time,
Going to meeting after meeting,
This revolution may never happen
And our time is far too fleeting."

But I find that mindset wrong,
For it doesn't understand
Revolution isn't some distant promise,
It's already here, in the palm of our hand

The revolution is now
If we can all just agree,
We will make the revolution happen
To save all humanity.

There won't be a TV broadcast
Where the news anchor will say,
"It's time for me to report,
The revolution starts today."

It begins when we decide it does
Because the revolution isn't abstract,
We are the revolution
And it starts when we decide to act.

Animal Rights

When cruelty is so engrained within a society it can be hard for those within that society to accept that there is cruelty. For to accept the cruelty of their society they must also accept their role in it, which is a difficult task.

Do not beat yourself up for things you did in the past when you weren't fully informed. But once you learn the truth you become able to make your own decision as to whether you want to partake in the cruelty, or to help prevent it.

Look into the eyes of a cow, and you will see the same spark of life that you see in cats, dogs and your fellow man.

Animal Rights

Children's Books - 29

Choice - 30

Chicken Run - 32

Animal Lovers - 33

Meat - 34

Humane Slaughter - 35

Vegetarian - 36

Vegan - 38

The Hard Truth - 40

Meat-eating Leftists - 41

Who Do We Blame? - 42

Think Of All The Animals - 43

Animal Rights | Opening Thoughts

Animal Rights is a topic that is not taken seriously enough by our society. The exploitation of animals is so normalised that it is no longer viewed as exploitation. I find it hard to even talk to people about what happens in the animal agriculture industry without them taking it as a personal attack.

I do not hate you because you eat meat. When I first went vegan I was very angry. I couldn't understand why people were doing something that was so obviously cruel. But then I realised, that I had spent the majority of my life doing the same thing.

The truth is that the "decision" to eat meat is not one that most of us make. It is one that is made for us as children, and then we grow up in a society that normalizes the practice, yet when most people start to think about what happened in order for meat to be made they feel sick.

Even within left wing circles, where people claim to want to end oppression and create a fairer society, people will justify the exploitation of animals using the same rhetoric that other groups use to justify the exploitation of human minorities.

I beg of you, please look into the realities of animal agriculture. For me it is the foundation of suffering upon which our society is built, and we will never achieve a utopian society until all living beings have rights, humans and animals.

Children's Books

We show young children
Books that spread lies,
Of cows in green fields
Beneath the blue skies.

We tell tales of a happy pig
Living on a happy farm,
A deception that's intended
To hide all the harm.

The books ease our guilt.
The books comfort our hearts.
They distract from the fact that
We eat body parts.

The propaganda we're shown
At such an early age,
The suffering is hidden
Not shown on the page.

We tell kids these lies
When we tuck them into bed.
For they don't need to know
That the food they were fed
Is the flesh of that happy pig,
Whose blood has been shed.

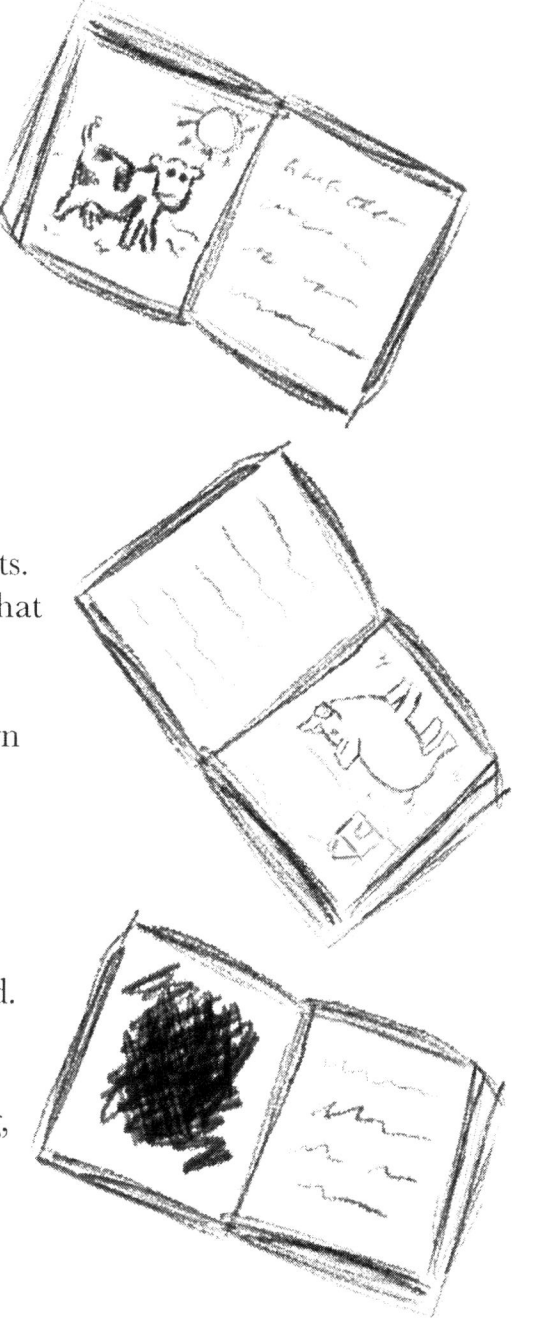

Choice

When did you decide you want to eat meat?
How did you make that decision?
Did you weigh up the options?
Consider your choices?

Or were you a baby?
Incapable of deciding,
Not truly understanding,
Your agency taken away.

Eating what you're given.
Eating what you're told.
Eating what you're parents ate.
Eating what is - "normal".

Kids read books about happy farm animals,
Teens are surrounded by ads perpetuating
the same lie,
And by the time you've grown up
You never got a chance to think.
The decision was never truly yours to make.

The adverts scream,
And the billboards declare
"YOU NEED MEAT"
The propaganda is everywhere.

Meat is sexy
Meat is power
Meat is status
Meat is right

Meat is normal
Meat is culture
Meat is tradition
Meat IS murder
BUT
Meat is "necessary" murder

Yet it's not too late

You never got to make a choice,
You never got to decide,
You have been programmed
But you don't have to obey.

The decision that was taken away
Is a decision you can always remake.

Learn the truth they tried to hide,
Think about the animals who for you have died,
Think about all the ways the industry has lied.

And when you do all that
The truth will be yours to see,
You can make your own choice
And take back your agency.

Chicken Run

When I was a kid
I loved Chicken Run.
I thought watching the film
Was very fun.

And while I watched it
I ate chicken pie,
Blissfully ignorant
That a bird had to die.

But now I'm an adult
I can finally see,
The villain of Chicken Run
Has always been me.

Animal Lovers

Animal lovers, animal lovers,
Love the cats like we're their mothers.

Animal lovers, animal lovers,
Turn their eyes while the cow suffers.

We love them cute and in our homes
But then we carve them to their bones.

We love the dogs because they're sweet
But kill the pigs so we can eat.

So learn the truth
You'll hate what you uncover,
But then you can decide
To truly be an animal lover.

Meat

I am a pig,
But all you see is pork.
I don't want to die,
Please spare me a thought.

I am a cow,
And I am a mother,
But you take away my baby
And leave me to suffer.

I am a chicken,
I can do lots of things.
But that doesn't matter to you,
You just want to eat my wings.

I have a soul
But that's not what you see.
You just see meat
And want to kill me.

Humane Slaughter

Humane Slaughter
What a joke
Humans laugh
While pigs choke

Humane slaughter
What a lie
Humans laugh
While animals die

Humane, humane
What a misused word
Gas the pig
And stab the bird

Humane, humane
Hide from the truth
Rape the mother
And kill her youth

The truth is slaughter
Is never humane
For the victims
Who feel the pain

And if you really
Want to be kind
Then open your eyes
Choose not to be blind

Vegetarian

You don't eat meat
And that is great
But you still put cheese
And eggs on your plate

I know your heart
Is in the right place
You wont eat anything
If it had a face

I don't want to sound mean
I don't want to sound cruel
And I know you don't really
Care for my approval

But please for a second
Just stop and think
Could there be something wrong
With the milk that you drink

"But for my milk
No one had to die!"
I can hear you say it
But I must reply

The truth behind milk
Is not so pretty
Look behind the facade
And you might start to pity

The mother cow,
Her baby taken away
So we can drink
Her milk today

If the baby's a girl
She'll be raised like her mother
But they won't ever get
To see one another

But if the baby's a boy
He can't makes us money
So we kill the child instead
Isn't that funny?

I know that you want
To do what's right
So think of the mother cow
Crying for her baby tonight

Vegan

I don't want to be
A vegan no more.
The truth is that
It's becoming a bore.

When people hear that
They act surprised,
Tell me I can't mean it
And must have just lied.

But it ain't a lie,
It's quite simply a fact.
That I don't know
If I can keep up this act.

I'm not trying to imply
Eating meat is what I desire.
But the whole vegan thing
Is starting to tire.

I don't want to eat eggs
And I don't crave cheese.
But I'm starting to feel
Like I have a disease.

I wish I wasn't special,
I wish I wasn't hated.
Just because I care that
Animals are being mutilated.

I wish that vegans
Had a better perception,
And I wish loving animals
Wasn't such an exception.

When I say I don't want to be vegan,
What I really mean to say,
Is that I wish there was no need for vegans
And the cruelty would all just go away.

So I'm proud to be a vegan,
I hope I can help you understand
I'll never stop fighting for the animals
And I pray you'll lend a hand

The Hard Truth

Every
Time
You
Eat
Meat
An
Animal
Was
Killed.

And
It
Didn't
Want
To
Die.

Meat-eating Leftists

I am against discrimination!
I think inequality is wrong!
I want to create a new world
Where everyone will belong.

I will die for my values!
And fight for those in need!
'Cause the sanctity of life
Is more important than greed.

But what about the animals
Who are killed for your food?
When it comes to your morals,
How do you choose who to include?

You say you'll speak for the voiceless,
And stand up for the defenseless,
But when it comes to the animals
Your logic is senseless.

How can you speak of injustice
While you continue to condemn
Innocent animals to slaughter.
Why won't you fight for them?

Who Do We Blame?

Who's responsible?
Who's to blame?
How do we assign,
Every killer their claim?

When the pigs are raised,
Just for us to eat.
Whose fault is it,
Their life's reduced to meat?

Can we blame the farmer,
Who brought them into this Earth?
Or maybe the slaughterhouse worker,
Whose actions were perverse?

Or perhaps the blame
Lies with another,
The child who wanted bacon
And their father and mother.

But is that too harsh?
Are they really to blame?
To call them killers,
Surely it's not the same?

But if we didn't continue
To buy meat from the store,
There wouldn't be any reason
For them to kill anymore.

Think Of All The Animals

Think of all the animals,
Of those without a voice.
Think of how they're suffering,
Before you make your choice.

Think of all the animals,
And think of how they died.
The packaging said it's all humane,
Perhaps the packaging lied?

Think of all the animals,
Some wild, some pets, some food.
Now swap them round and eat your pets
- am I being crude?

Think of all the animals,
Picture them in your mind.
Now it's time to make your choice,
Will you choose to be kind?

Climate Change

Climate change is perhaps the most blatant example of how the interests of capitalism and the interests of humanity are not aligned. Our planet is dying but it is not profitable to save it.

It isn't profitable to save ourselves.

Climate Change

Ignore The Scientists - 53

Thinking About My Grandkids - 54

Recycling - 55

Keep Throwing Soup At Paintings - 56

Activists - 57

Green - 58

Time - 59

Sleepwalking - 60

Beauty - 61

Climate Change | Opening Thoughts

I feel climate change is the perfect example of how interlinked all of these topics are.

Large corporations were the first to know about the impact they were having on the environment and the long-term effects it would have on our planet. And their response?

Cover it up and deflect the blame.

The industries that are most detrimental to the planet happen to be very profitable, and the people who own those industries have the money, the power and the resources to protect their investments, even if their investments are destroying our planet.

Animal agriculture is one of the most harmful industries when it comes to environmental impact. But big money is invested in animal agriculture, so a transition to a more ethical, environmentally friendly way of living will be restricted to protect those investments.

Capitalism cannot solve the climate crisis, as the climate crisis is a symptom of capitalism.

Climate change is to the earth what capitalism is to the worker.

Ignore The Scientists

Ignore the scientitists,
See through their disguise.
They don't know what they're saying,
They're just spreading lies.

They're just speading fear
And needless confusion.
Pay no attention
To their shared delusion.

The tests are faulty!
The results are flawed!
They are all biased,
And guilty of fraud!

Don't start to question,
Don't start to doubt,
We've got it all sorted!
We've got it all figured out!

Ignore the scientists,
Silence their cries.
We need to make money
Even if the planet dies.

Thinking About My Grandkids

Sometimes I wonder
What my grandkids will learn,
How will we tell them
We let the world burn?

Sometimes I fear
What my grandkids will say,
"Why didn't you do something
To stop the trees going away?"

Sometimes I think
That my grandkids will hate
The fact we did nothing
'Til it was too late.

My grandkids will ask
"Why didn't you stop it?"
And I will reply,
"All we cared for was profit"

Recycling

Recycling is great!
But it won't stop climate change.
Yet they stress its importance,
Isn't that strange?

Recycling is really
A massive distraction,
To prevent us from taking
Proper climate action.

So keep recycling
But pay attention
To how rarely the news
Gives big oil's impact a mention.

Keep Throwing Soup At Paintings

Keep throwing soup at paintings
Keep glueing yourself to the road
Keep pissing off the oil companies
And making their oil pipes explode

Activists

Activists are trying
To make the public see
That the Earth is crying
As we cut down every tree

The companies are lying
So they can make money
Our planet is dying
Yet we don't act urgently

Green

Nature's beauty;
Trees
Bushes
Leaves

Stands unappreciated.

Slowly being
Lost
Replaced
Cut down

The green of nature,
A thing of the past

Gutted, bled and pulped
Transformed and ruined

The green of today,
The note in the hand

No longer admired,
Is the beauty of the tree.
Instead man admires
Its corpse, his ugly money.

Time

It's funny how time
Can move so fast,
Yet our society remains
So stuck in the past.

Minutes turn to hours
And hours into days,
But we can't seem to move on
From our old ways.

As humans we have
Such great potential,
Yet we act like our survival
Isn't essential.

So treasure every minute
And seize every day,
Let's make sure we spend them
Fighting for a better way.

The Earth is slowly dying,
Now's not the time for debate.
We must act now
Or it'll be too late.

Sleepwalking

Our world stands on the edge,
Hastily approaching our demise,
Yet we all seem so determined
To never open our eyes.

With every passing hour,
We continue to seal our fate.
If we don't soon stop our sleepwalking
It will soon become too late.

Sometimes I curse my knowledge
And envy those whose eyes are closed.
Why suffer the pain of knowing
When our enemy stands unopposed.

I wish I knew the answer
To wake up everyone,
But sadly no one listens
As what I say isn't fun.

I plead you now to join me,
Try to spread the word.
Sleepwalking into annihilation,
The whole thing seems absurd.

Beauty

Our oceans are filled with plastic,
Our landscapes are hidden by trash.
We ignore disaster coming,
We're distracted by the cash.

Slowly nature's place is lost,
A relic of the past.
We seem to be preparing,
Nature's role being recast.

But the beauty of our planet
Should not be left behind.
Our forests are so beautiful,
How is man so blind?

Ugly buildings built by man,
Beauty not the goal.
Cost-efficient architecture,
Humanity's sold its soul.

Yet the Earth ignores us,
Our planet makes life art
Its beauty flowing eternal
As it has done from the start.

Despite rising sea levels,
And despite every burning tree,
The sun still rises every morning
To shine a light on our planets beauty.

LGBT Rights

Love is the most beautiful part of our existence, and yet our society has constantly tried to undermine that beauty. We have tried to categorise, control and limit a complex natural feeling.

Don't let anyone else tell you how or who to love. Let love be your guide in all your endeavours, and express it however you choose.

LGBT Rights

Gay Or Straight - 71

A Date With A Man - 72

Gender - 75

I Love My Trans Friends - 76

Gay - 77

Stop Talking About Bathrooms - 80

Love - 81

LGBT Rights | Opening Thoughts

My first memories of the word "gay" are of it being used as an insult. A word used by boys at school to mock those who were bad at sports or enjoyed more feminine things. When I learned what the word really meant, that first impression still lingered in my head.

LGBT people have been demonized throughout history, and this is seen today with horrific attacks against the trans community. We have seen a lot of significant leaps forward for LGBT rights in the last couple of decades, but there is still a lot of work to be done.

Across the globe people are still being killed just for loving who they love. How can we sit by and allow this to happen?

In our own country, trans children are killing themselves because they don't feel seen. How can we sit by and allow this to happen?

Gay or Straight

When I was a kid
I thought you had to choose
You like men or women
The other you refuse

It was quite simple
The world's black and white
But I felt lost
And that didn't sound right

I didn't know
If I was straight or gay
I thought I liked both
But thought it wasn't ok

And when I found out
Liking both is allowed
I finally came out
And now I am proud

A Date With A Man

When I was younger
I had a date with a man.
It was rather spontaneous,
Wasn't much of a plan.

We went out for dinner,
Then went for a drink.
This is going well
I started to think.

We had lots of laughs,
I felt we had a connection.
When I looked in his eyes
So much sexual tension.

But things took a turn
When a group of men came in.
That's when the trouble
Started to begin.

They started to shout
Such horrible things.
I wish it didn't hurt
But the memory still stings.

The man I was with
Said "It'll be ok".
And in that moment
I felt so gay.

So we tried to ignore them
And have a nice night
But in the back of my mind
I was scared of a fight.

But it wouldn't be a fight,
More of a beating.
Just because it was a man
With whom I was eating.

I went to the bathroom,
That's when it went wrong.
When I was made to feel
Like I'd never belong.

One of the guys
Was in there as well,
And he looked at me like
He'd send me to hell.

I bumped into him,
It was just a mistake.
He shoved me to the ground
And I started to ache.

I feared what would happen,
A punch or a kick?
But it wasn't that bad,
It was over quite quick.

He turned to me,
Stared me dead in the eye,
Shouted "Fuck off faggot"
And I feared I might die.

But then the man left
With me still on the floor,
I'd never felt so ashamed
Of being gay before.

So I started to cry,
Head full of shame,
Until the man I was with
Started calling my name.

I pulled myself up,
Told him I had to leave.
Couldn't admit what had happened
So I chose to deceive.

When I was lying
In my bed that night,
I couldn't stop thinking
My sexuality wasn't right.

"Fuck off faggot"
I bet he felt clever.
"Fuck off faggot"
Will haunt me forever.

Gender

Gender isn't real,
Can we stop pretending.
This shared delusion
Seems never-ending.

I say I'm a man
Cause I don't want to explain,
That thinking about gender
Hurts my brain.

I Love My Trans Friends

I love my trans friends,
And think they're so brave.
I hate how our government,
Wants them in a grave.

I love my trans friends,
For living their truth.
I'll always believe you,
I'll never need proof.

I love my trans friends,
I hope they know they belong.
I'm here for you always,
Even when the world feels so wrong.

Gay

I remember when
I was younger
I was in school
I was confused

"He's gay"
The other kids would say
A claim which I denied
Not thinking I had lied

Gay is a bad word
Used to offend
Weaponized by kids who
Don't really understand

"You're gay" they say
"I'm not" (I hope not)
But why is gay bad again?

I remember when
I was a bit older
I was still in school
I was still confused

"I'm gay"
My friend told me
Then I'm sworn to secrecy
He's scared of the world's reaction

Gay is no longer a bad word
At least it shouldn't be
But I can't be gay
Surely I would've known by now

My friend says he always knew
But the teasing made him hide it
Surely I would've known by now

I remember when
I was even older
I was still in school
I was no longer confused

"I'm gay"
Now I'm the one speaking
But I still have a weird feeling
I only tell it to the mirror

Gay is a proud word
You shouldn't feel any shame
I know this is true
But I hide it anyway

I know it's not a problem
But the teasing left a mark
That I can't remove from my heart

Where I am today
I'm quite a bit older
I'm no longer in school
I'm no longer confused

"I'm gay"
Yet again it is my voice
But now it is my choice
To tell people not just mirrors

Gay is love
I feel it in my heart
To some it might not mean that
And I think that's a real shame

Because gay or straight it doesn't matter
Love is the most beautiful thing
And to use who someone loves as an insult
I find rather baffling

Stop Talking About Bathrooms

Stop talking about bathrooms
Like you even care,
That's not why you're mad
And you're well aware.

You just hate the fact
Trans people exist
But they're here to stay
And they will resist.

Because you're just a bigot
And you're just a crook,
So go to the mirror
And take a second look.

And if you do that
Then maybe you'll see,
Trans people aren't so different
From you and from me.

Love

In a world that is divided,
And seems so full of hate.
It can be easy to forget
What makes humanity great.

Our greatest superpower,
The thing that keeps us strong.
It can bring us all together,
Make a world where we all belong.

Try to listen to your heart,
And when push comes to shove.
The answers rather simple,
Always follow love.

Mental Health

Our societal view on mental health is that mental health issues arise due to problems with an individual, be they genetic or situational.

While this may be true, I find it unlikely that the rise in mental health issues is solely because of problems with the individual, as opposed to a symptom of much larger societal problems being unaddressed.

Depressed people spend more to try and distract from their suffering. Our society depresses us by design.

Mental Health

Tough Day - 91

Clown - 92

Anxiety - 93

Men Have Emotions - 94

Memory - 95

Tortured Poet - 96

Self-Harm - 97

I Really Don't Want To Die - 98

Breakdown - 101

Numb - 102

Train - 103

The Voice - 104

Descent - 106

The Heart - 107

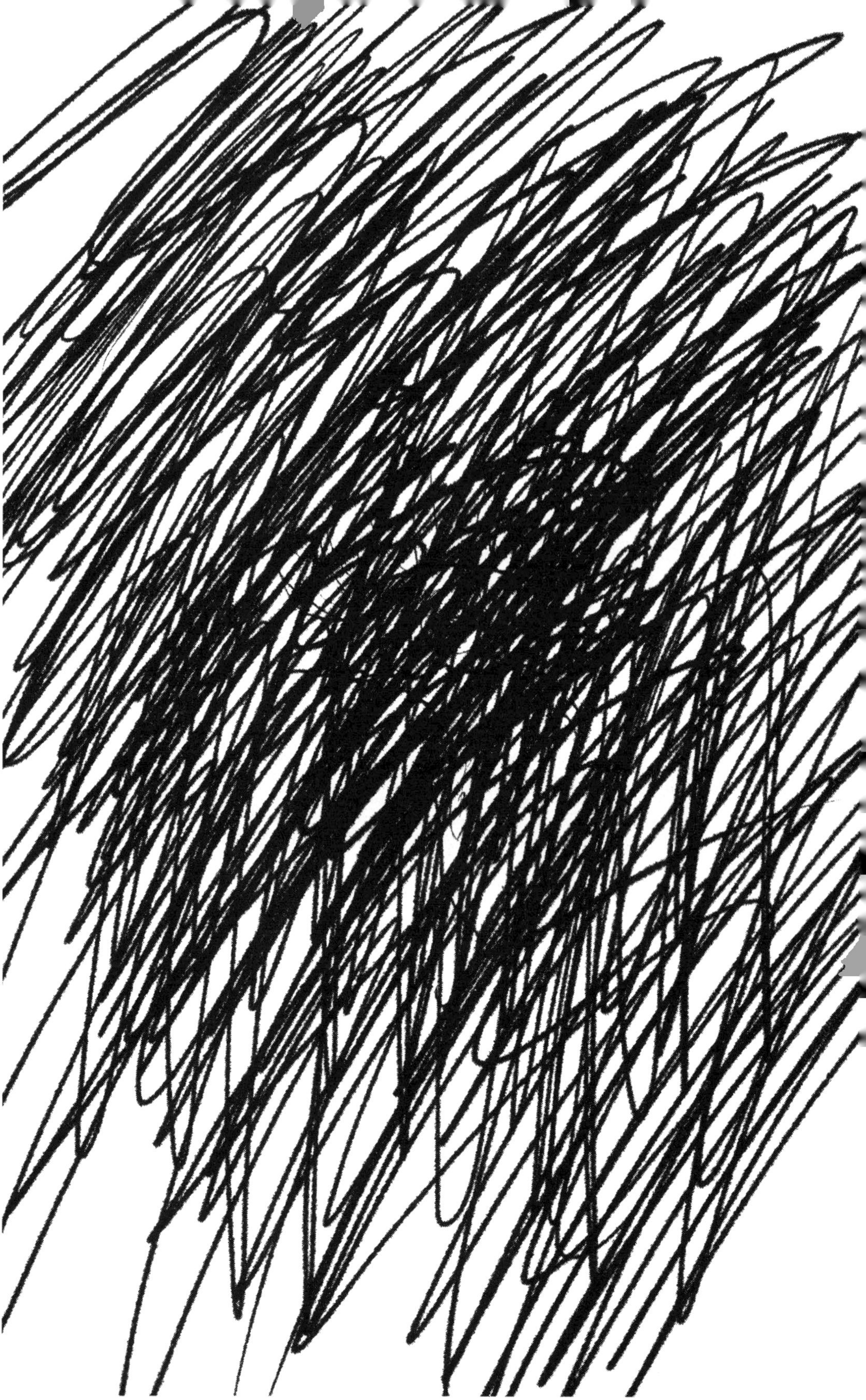

Mental Health | Opening Thoughts

To anyone who is struggling with depression, anxiety or suicidal thoughts, the only thing I can say to you is that it does get better, and that there are people out there who care for you.

I know it sounds cliche, and I know you don't believe me. But I promise you its true.

I didn't believe it when I would hear it. Sometimes I knew that people loved me but at that moment it didn't matter because the pain inside was so overwhelming and it felt like it would never go away.

But it did. And then it came back. And it came back again, and it came back worse.

But now I'm on the other side. I know that I will probably go back to that dark place again, but I'm not scared of that anymore. Because I know I have a circle of people around me who are there for me.

And even if you feel like you don't have that, I promise you that there are people out there who are waiting to love you. You just have to let them in.

Our societal understanding of mental health has progressed massively, but it still has a long way to go.

This "epidemic of depression" hasn't come from nowhere. It is a symptom of living in a society that treats people as if they are nothing more than a cog in a machine.

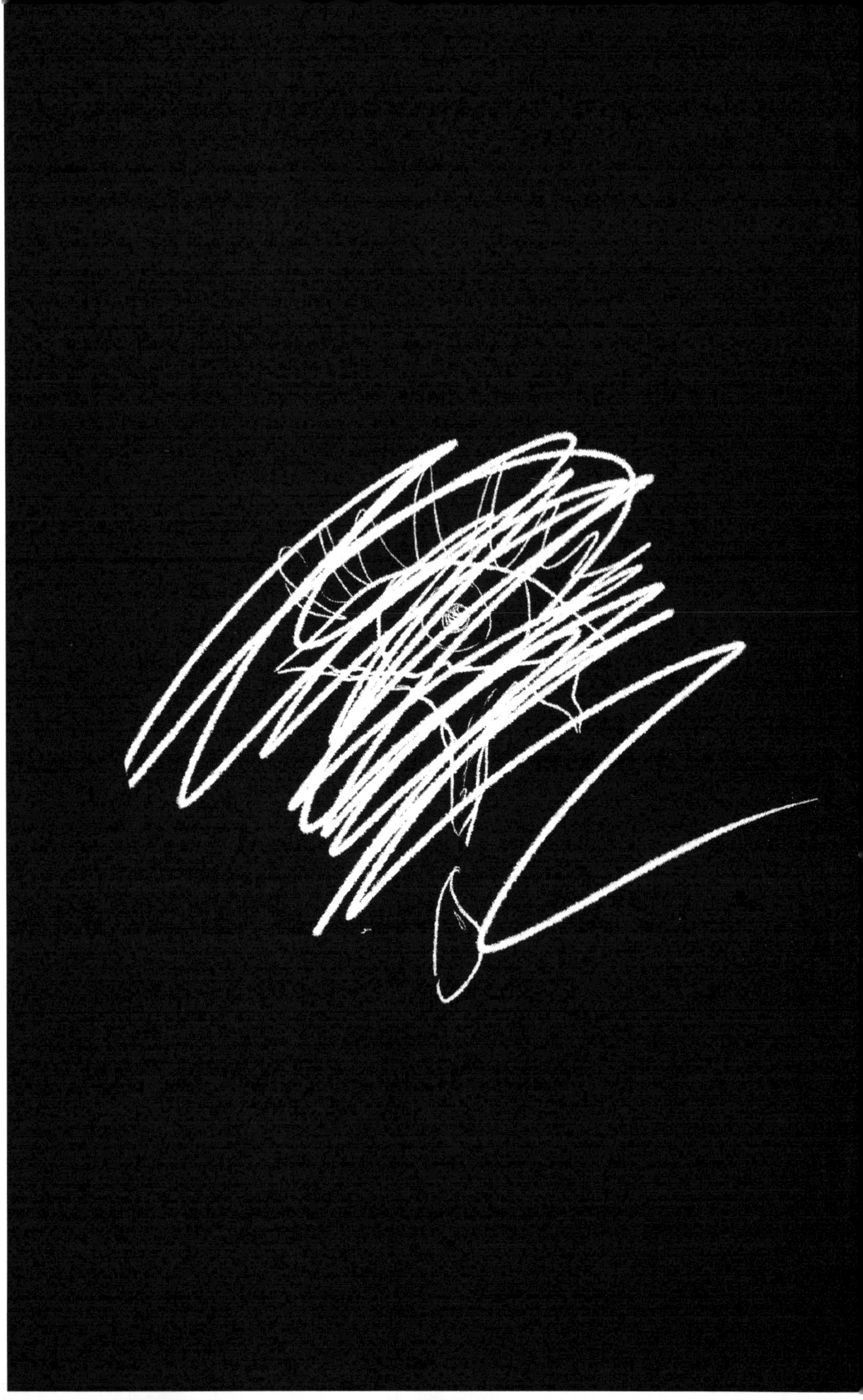

Tough Day

It's been a tough day,
But that's not a problem.
Not every day can be perfect,
Tomorrow will be ok.

Another tough day,
That's two in a row,
But things will get better,
You'll stop feeling so low.

It's been a tough week,
Keep your head up.
Next week you'll have
Your winning streak.

It's been a tough month,
But things will get better.
Things can't be
This bad forever.

It's been a tough year,
Can't keep lying to myself.
It might never get better,
And that's what I fear.

Things have been tough
For far too long.
Don't know if I
Can keep trying to be strong.

Clown

I'll just make a joke,
Because I can't cope,
The laughter's a cloak,
Hiding my fading hope.

Always wearing a smile,
But it's always fake.
Haven't been happy in a while,
I can't catch a break.

The laughs are lies
That are meant
To try and disguise
My quickening descent.

I can never admit
When I'm feeling down,
Hide it with my wit
Cause I'm just a clown.

Anxiety

Does anyone like me?
Does anyone care?
Who ever said
Life had to be fair?

Are they staring?
What do they think?
Feel like I'm in water
And I'm starting to sink.

You're so UGLY!
You're so FAT!
You look so STUPID,
In that hat!

You're friends pretend,
That you are great
But really all
They feel is HATE

I really want
To run and hide
Maybe it'd be better
If I just died.

Men Have Emotions

Men have emotions,
Sometimes they even cry.
We need to normalize this now,
Or countless men will die.

It's ok for men to be scared,
It's ok for men to be sad.
You can be scared as a child,
And still be scared as a dad.

So normalize these emotions,
And tell your friends you care.
Because if we don't do this now,
One day they might not be there.

Memory

I feel like I should
Remember more than I do.
I wish that I could
Remember what's true.

It's like there's a leak
Inside of my brain.
I feel like a freak
Being driven insane.

I can't remember my past,
I can't remember being a child.
It was over so fast,
My memories have been misfiled.

My memories are fleeting,
My memories are gone.
My past is retreating,
My memory is withdrawn.

Tortured Poet

Tortured poet, tortured poet
You think you're smart
And we all know it.

Tortured poet, tortured soul
Stop pitying yourself
And get out of that hole.

Tortured poet, tortured fool
Your shitty poems
Don't make you cool.

Oh boo hoo
You had a hard life,
That doesn't make you special
So put down the knife.

Self-Harm

I sometimes forget
I used to self harm
But then I look
At the scars on my arm
And I remember
It made me feel so calm

I start to feel sick
Knowing what I used to do
"I'll never do it again"
And I hope that that's true
I think of my past self
And whisper "I love you"

I Really Don't Want To Die

I really, really
Don't want to die,
And I promise
That isn't a lie.

When I think of death
I get so scared,
I start to feel
So unprepared.

But sometimes life
Is just too much,
And I start to crave
Death's sweet touch.

My mind is filled
With a screaming voice
Telling me
"You have no choice"

"You have to die"
"There's no other way"
"Kill yourself Ryan"
"Do it today"

But like I said
I really don't want to.
But then the voice says
"No one loves you"

The voice is so loud
I can't hear myself.
The voice takes over,
I grab the noose from the shelf.

I really really
Don't want to die,
But sometimes I wonder
Could that be a lie?

Why do I bother
Keeping on living
When life can be
So unforgiving.

What is true?
And what is not?
I desperately cling
To the little sanity I've got.

I try to say
"Everything will be ok"
But the voice replies
"You're telling lies"

I want to live!
I really do!
I just need to try
Something new.

But the voice is relentless,
It won't give in.
The battle ain't over,
I don't think I can win.

I can't live for myself,
That hasn't worked before.
So I think of my friends
Who I adore.

If I can't live for me
Because of my own self hatred,
Then I'll do it for
The people that I hold sacred.

And as I think
Of the people I cherish,
The voice is weakened
And it starts to perish.

The fight is over,
But only for today.
I know it won't be forever,
The Voice never goes away.

A Breakdown

I'm feeling low,
What to do?
Oh, I know!
I'll go to my room.

I'll write a poem
And pour out my heart,
It won't change the world
But it'll be a start.

But I stared at the page
And it remained blank,
My mind filled with rage
And then my heart sank

"You think your poems
Can change the world?"

They won't

Your poems are terrible

You are terrible

This is terrible

Don't publish this

You are terrible

Kill yourself tomorrow

Numb

I used to think of numb
As an absence
A lack of feeling
A void
A hole
An emptiness

But now I realise
Numb is not a lack of feeling
Instead
Numb is constant exposure
Numb is all the emotions at once
An overload
A bombardment of feelings
A thundering storm

Numb is not when you feel nothing
Numb is when you feel so much
That you can't process the feelings

Train

Sometimes I can't
Get it out of my brain,
The overwhelming urge
To jump in front of a train.

I stand and wait
On the platform,
While inside my mind
There's a gathering storm.

Now I can see
The approaching train
And I hear The Voice
Inside my brain
"If you jump,
There'll be no more pain"

Inside my chest
I feel my heart pump
I get the urge…

… but I don't jump

I'm suddenly hit
By a wave of relief,
But if I had jumped
The pain would have been brief…

The Voice

Alone I stand
At the edge of the canyon.
Alone except for The Voice,
My unwanted companion.

I can't remember a time
Before The Voice.
Criticising every decision,
Criticising every choice.

Feeling a little sad?
The Voice is there,
To turn this sadness
Into utter despair.

Feeling happy?
Not for long,
The Voice will ensure
Everything goes wrong.

The Voice will leave
To give false hope,
But then it returns
With thoughts of the rope.

The Voice is here
And it's here to stay,
If you want it gone
There is only one way.

It whispers, murmurs,
Screams and shouts
All your fears,
And all your doubts.

I know I'm loved
But The Voice will deny,
The Voice won't stop
Until I die.

Is The Voice me?
It's inside my head -
Do I really want
To see myself dead?

Or could it be a demon?
Or some devilish ghoul?
With its own motivations
So evil and cruel.

The Voice knows no reason,
The Voice doesn't care.
The Voice is always
Going to be there.

Alone I stand
At the edge of the canyon.
Alone except for The Voice
That I hope to abandon.

Descent

Sometimes my mental health improves
And I start to feel good about myself.
It's like I have been given a chance,
Another chance to start again.
But it doesn't last very long,
Slowly it all slips away,
Until I find myself
At the bottom
Of that pit
Sad and
Alone

But,
Slowly,
I start to
Get back up.
Piece by piece
I find myself again.
The dark feels eternal,
But the light always returns.

The Heart

A bleeding heart lies in a pit,
Tears flow from its veins.
In that pit it wallows,
Suffering through its pains.

That heart has been discarded,
Trampled, beaten, bruised.
The man who used to own it,
Finds himself confused.

The heart had caused him misery,
Kept him up at night.
But now he is without it,
Still doesn't feel alright.

He quickly rushes to the pit,
And takes his heart in hand.
This isn't what he wanted,
This isn't what he planned.

He puts the heart back in his chest
And feels the pain again.
Yet the pain is different now,
Its powers start to wane.

A lesson learned the hard way,
He knows now what is true.
Pain can't truly be repressed
The only way out is through.

Addiction

Addiction gets you slowly. Bit by bit it breaks your barriers until you find yourself looking in the mirror and not recognising the reflection.

When you struggle to regulate your emotions in this crazy messed up world, addiction offers comfort.

But as you delve ever deeper into its trap, the comfort fades and the horrors become worse than the things you were trying to escape.

Addiction

Drugs Are Bad - 117

Maybe - 118

Everybody Loves Me - 120

Liar - 121

KETAMINE - 122

One More - 123

Passenger - 124

Drinking - 125

Fun - 126

Meetings - 127

Sober - 128

Relapse - 129

The Demon Inside - 130

Moment Of Truth - 131

Addiction

What I learned about drugs as a child was very different from the truth I discovered as a teen. I grew up believing that if you did any drug once, you would become instantly addicted and your life would be ruined.

So when I went to university, and met several people who seemed to have their lives a lot more together than I did, I was shocked to find out that a lot of them used drugs recreationally. What I had been taught about drugs did not match up with reality.

I realised my education around drugs had been wrong. Misinformation used to scare kids away. But the problem with this is that once I saw past the fearmongering, it was hard to see the actual warning signs.

In order to prevent addiction our societal understanding of drugs has to change. We need actual drug education instead of fearmongering so that people can make informed decisions.

Drugs aren't good or bad. Drugs just are. It's our relationship with them that can be good or bad. That is true of all drugs, even the societally acceptable ones like alcohol - which is truthfully a lot more dangerous than a lot of the substances that are illegal.

Drugs Are Bad

When I was a kid
I was told drugs are bad.
My mum liked to smoke,
And that made me sad.

Doing drugs is stupid,
Doing drugs is dumb.
If you do drugs once,
You'll become a homeless bum.

Drug addicts are worthless,
LAZY!
STUPID!
MEAN!

Drug addicts are idiots,
Who don't know how to clean.

When I was a kid,
I made a promise to myself.
I will never do any drugs,
And I'll take good care of my health.

I broke that promise

I don't know why

But I did

Maybe

Maybe I'll try it.
Just a little,
Just once.
Just for this extra special occasion.

Maybe you like it.
Maybe you'll do it again.
But not for a while,
Not until that next extra special occasion.

It's been a month,
You deserve a treat.
It's been a while,
Ah what the hell.

You do it at a party,
You do it with friends.
It's fun, It's a laugh.
Everyone's smiling, You're smiling.

It's been a week,
You're feeling a bit down.
Just this once,
Take it on your own.

Every weekend,
That's ok.
Some people drink,
We all have our vices.

Every day,
But just after work.
You have to have limits,
You have to have rules.

Hard day - Very hard day.
Lunch break,
Do it then.
Everything's ok.

Everyday,
Every lunch break.
No escape.
Not ok.

Not ok

Everybody Loves Me

Everyone loves me
Because I'm such fun.
Everyone loves me
I feel like number one.

Everyone loves me
But why can't they see,
Get rid of the drugs
And you get rid of me.

Liar

I'm getting better - I say
That's what they want to hear.
They'll hate me if they know
And that's what I fear.

Lie to your loved one,
Lie to your friend.
You're a liar now Ryan,
You'll lie 'til the end.

It's not what you want,
But addiction doesn't care.
Everyone's a liar
When caught in its snare.

KETAMINE

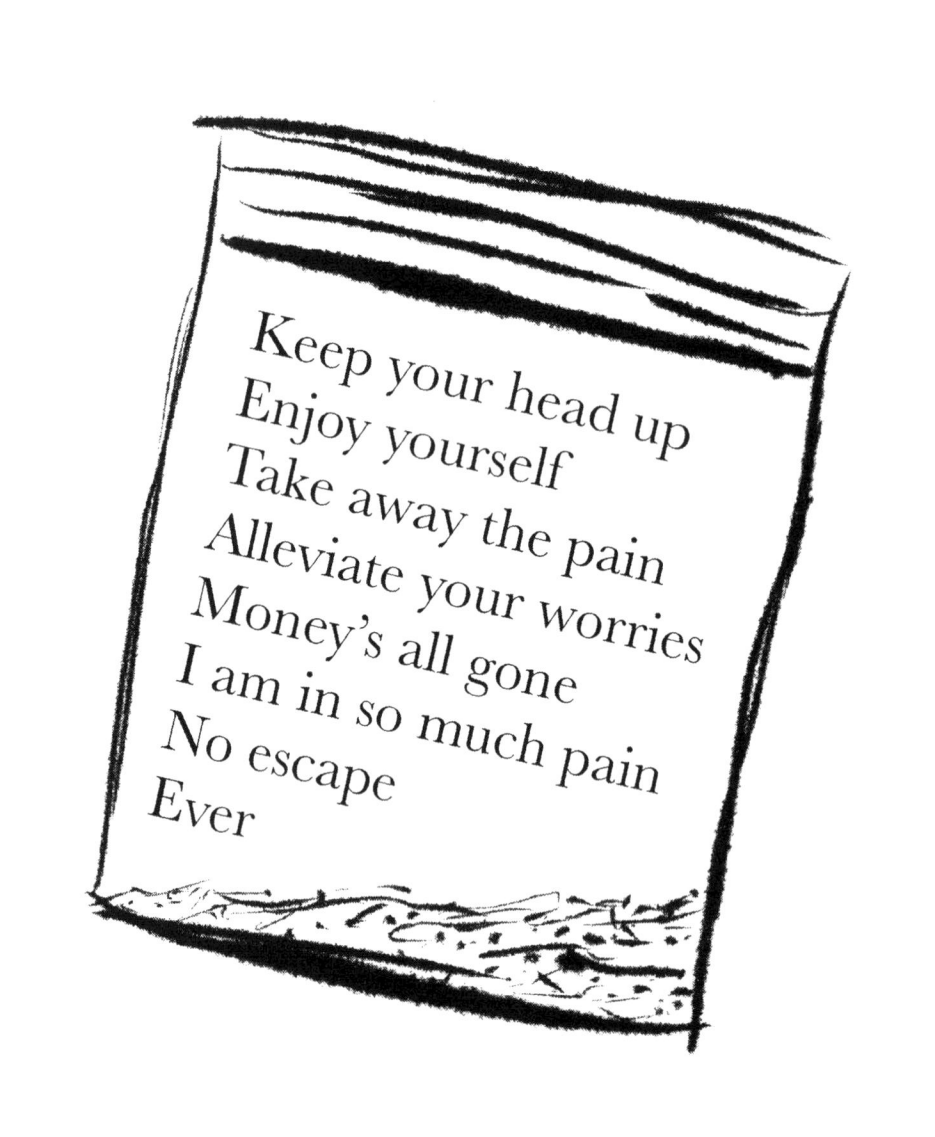

Keep your head up
Enjoy yourself
Take away the pain
Alleviate your worries
Money's all gone
I am in so much pain
No escape
Ever

One More

One more line,
One more bag,
One more bump,
One more fag.

One more hit,
One more joint,
One more needle,
What's the point?

It's never going to be
Just one more,
So stop lying to yourself
It's becoming a bore.

Passenger

Sometimes I feel
Like I'm not in control.
My body is moving
But it disobeys my soul.

I don't want to smoke,
I don't want to drink.
But I do it on instinct,
I don't even think.

Why won't I stop?
I wish that I knew.
I say I'll stop soon
But I doubt that that's true.

I scream at myself
To stop it all now
But for some reason I can't
Seem to figure out how.

Drinking

Drinking is normal!
Drinking is fun!
If you don't have a drink,
Then you're the weird one!

Isn't it strange
That drugs are so bad,
But alcohol's a drug
And if you don't drink it you're mad.

The truth is, my friend,
That alcohol is behind
Just as much harm
As the other drugs you can find.

Fun

Drugs are fun!
Addiction is not.
When you're addicted
Your mind starts to rot.

You'll snap at your friends,
You'll stop being yourself.
Say goodbye to your credit,
And goodbye to your health.

Addiction makes you different,
Addiction makes you change.
Your friends will find you creepy,
Your friends will find you strange.

So do drugs for fun
But please take care,
Bcause addiction will come
Out of nowhere.

Meetings

Week after week
I go to the meetings,
But it's all just smiles
And pleasant greetings.

How many meetings
Do I have to attend
For this addiction
To finally end?

Progress is slow
And I keep failing.
I wish this journey
Would be smooth sailing.

They say trust in the process
But I can't even trust me,
I hope that sometime soon
I have the strength to set myself free.

Sober

So many thoughts
Fill my mind,
I don't know
How to unwind.

For so long
All I'd do,
Bury the pain
Don't push through.

Now I'm sober
I can't stop,
Over a cliff
I'm gonna drop.

Sober is hard,
There's no way
I can take
The pain away.

Relapse

Another day
I'm doing good
Everything
Will be ok

Another day
I'm staying clean
Everything
Will be ok

Another day
Bit of a struggle
But everything
Will be ok

Another day
I start to doubt
If everything
Will be ok

I mess up
And start to feel
Like nothing
Will be ok

The Demon Inside

Inside of my mind
There are two fighting souls.
One of them's a good man,
The other burns children with coals.

You have the version
That I want to be,
He's kind and he's caring
I hope that's who you see.

But then there's the monster
Who hides in my brain,
He doesn't care about my friends
Even if they're in pain.

All that he wants
And all that he knows,
Is that he needs to shove
Drugs up his nose.

Moment Of Truth

So now the bag's empty,
Time to face the fire.
Will I stay true to my promise
Or turn into a liar.

I know that deep down
I want it all to stop,
But there's a fight happening inside me
And the demon always ends up on top.

But this time is different
I know it to be true.
I think of my friends,
I'm doing it for you.

Palestine

Do not allow what is happening to be called anything other than what it is. A genocide.

The Western world is to be blamed. We are the ones who started this, and we are the ones who sit back and do nothing while countless people are killed.

Never forget what Israel are doing, and never forget our leaders' complicity.

Free Palestine

الحرية لفلسطين

Palestine

Channel Surfing - 123

Detached - 124

Luxuries - 125

Prayer For Gaza - 126

Terrorist - 127

Politicians - 128

"Anti-Semite" - 129

Scared - 130

What Happened Before - 131

Conversation - 132

Palestine | Opening Thoughts

History will not look kindly on us. Countless children dead yet we can't say the word genocide.

Not only do we refuse to condemn Israel but we continue to support it.

Everyone knows what is happening. Even those who won't admit it. And yet I feel powerless to enact any real change.

We are living our lives while a genocide is happening and they expect us to carry on like business as usual.

I wish I could be optimistic but I fear for the worst.

Never stop talking about Palestine. Don't let it fall out of the public consciousness.

What Israel are doing is wrong. What we are doing is wrong.

Channel Surfing

" Good morning and welcome to - "
      " - AND HE SCORES! PUTTING - "
" - in its natural habitat - "
      " - the death toll continues to - "
" - it's been a big week for - "
      " - available at all good - "
" - protestors are being beaten - "
      " - wedding of pop sensation - "
" - to cook this at home you'll need - "
      " - children are dying of starvation - "
" - and then add 3 cloves of garlic - "
" - proving to be a difficult race for - "
      " - donate now and you can help - "
" - have invaded Rafah earlier - "
      " - if you're worried about your mental - "
" - the Israeli government is guilty of - "
      " - unexpected turn of events has resulted - "
" - second place goes to - "
      " - as for the weather in the south expect - "
" - bombs continue to rain on Gaza - "
" - that's all for tonight, see you again tomorrow."

Detatched

I wake up
I walk to work
I open up the shop
I greet the customers
I make them their coffee
I give them their cake
I talk to them about their lives
I clean the tables
I mop the floors
I close the shop

And while I'm doing my safe daily routine

In the back of my mind

All I can think of is the genocide

And my inability to do anything to stop it.

Luxuries

The things we take for granted,
That others would give so much for.
The luxuries of privilege,
The unappreciated necessities.

I never wake up worried
About where I'll get my water.
Have a long shower,
Don't think anything of it.

My phone charges,
My light turns on.
Never a doubt,
Why wouldn't they?

I ignore a call from my dad,
I can call him back tomorrow.
I don't spare a thought for those
Who would give all they have
Just to hear the sound
Of their fathers' voice.

Prayer For Gaza

I'm not religious
So I don't often pray,
But for the people in Gaza
I'll make an exception today.

I pray to a God
Whose existence I doubt,
I haven't prayed in a while
Should I whisper or shout?

I'll pray on behalf
Of all the Palestinian mothers
Who've lost their daughters
And their daughters' brothers.

I'll pray that one day
This genocide will end,
But I fear my prayer will be unheard.
So I leave it with you God,
On you I depend.

Terrorist

Isn't it funny
That when you resist
Your own occupation
You're labelled a terrorist.

We bomb their hospitals,
We bomb their schools.
Yet when they label us villains,
We say they are fools.

But when kicked out their homes
And told they don't belong,
How is it the Palestinians
Who are in the wrong?

Politicians

Our politicians are cowards
For they have denied
To call what's happening in Gaza
A needless genocide.

All that politicians
Really care for
Is money and power
And they always want more.

Our politicians don't care
About doing what's right.
People are dying
But they'll stay silent tonight.

"Anti-Semite"

"If you oppose Israel
Then you must hate all the Jews"
A horrid lie, and nothing more
Propagated by our news

There are Jewish voices on our side
Speaking out against your brutality
Israel doesn't speak for the Jewish people
And that is just reality

Because Jewish, Muslim, White or Black
The truth is clear for all to see
You are committing a genocide
While trying to gain our sympathy

Scared

I used to get scared
When I was a child,
Of vampires and werewolves
Out there in the wild.

I used to have nightmares,
I used to have fears.
But then I woke up
And the terror disappears.

But for the children in Gaza
That isn't the case.
Their monsters are real
And they look them in the face.

They aren't scared of ghosts,
They're scared of the bombs.
They aren't scared of clowns,
They're scared of losing their mums.

I couldn't see it then,
But it's now so obvious to me,
That my pitiful fears
Were in fact a luxury.

What Happened Before

On October 7th
Gaza started a war.
No need to look
At what happened before.

Please don't Google
The Balfour Decloration,
If it was important
It'd have been in your education.

No need to learn
What the Nakba means,
Just pay attention
To what's on your TV screens.

What does the word
Intifada mean?
Who even cares
Just have some caffeine!

We will make sure
The problems go away,
So just remember
To trust what we say.

On October 7th
Gaza started a war.
No need to look
At what happened before.

Conversation

I had a conversation
With a dear friend
And he asked me when
Would this genocide end

It was with regret
That I replied
I fear it won't stop
Until all the Palestinians have died

Of course I hope
That that's not true
But our world leaders' actions
Have informed my view

The only hope I have
That I might be wrong
Is that the people stay loud
And the people stay strong

Because the people are clear
They want Palestine to be free
And we won't stop our protests
Until the Palestinians have safety

War

HERE LIES THE GRAVES OF THE POOR WHO DIED SO THE RICH COULD GET RICHER.

We are sold a lie of brave men sacrificing their lives for their country. It is true that they were brave, but their lives weren't sacrificed for their country, they were sacrificed so that rich men could get richer.

I do not wish to disrespect the lives of the brave soldiers whose lives were needlessly lost, but instead I wish to disrespect the lives of the people who sent them.

War

Death For Profit - 159

How Much? - 160

Chess - 161

Children - 162

Artists At War - 163

Pawns For The Rich - 164

Remember - 165

War | Opening Thoughts

The decision to go to war is not made by those whose lives are sacrificed. Those who gain the most from war are the least affected by it, and those who are most affected gain nothing.

When I was younger I considered joining the army. I wanted to be brave, I wanted to be strong and I wanted to protect my country. This is what we are taught is the reason we have an army.

I still have a lot of respect for soldiers, both those who died before and those who are fighting now. But I also have a lot of sympathy.

Military propaganda is everywhere, it is so commonplace it goes unnoticed.

The poor are fodder for the rich. Just pieces in their game.

Death For Profit

Death for profit
Makes life a joke.
How much would it cost
For you to stab this bloke?

Making money from murder
Doesn't seem fair,
And the soldiers who die
Never see their share.

The ones who make millions
Don't even fight.
Instead they lie safely
In their beds at night.

Isn't it funny
The way wars are fought,
The ending of life
Is something to be bought.

How Much?

How much is a gun?
How much is a knife?
How much is a bullet?
How much is a life?

How much is a tank?
How much is a bomb?
How much is a soldier
Whose birth name was Tom?

How do we decide,
How much things cost?
And when was the value
Of life truly lost?

Who has the nerve
To ever say,
"Your son will die
But we will pay?"

Chess

Chess is fun
But chess is a game,
Actual war
Is never so tame.

You sacrifice pieces
Like you sacrifice men,
But the pieces are nameless
This soldier was called Ben.

When the game ends
One player has won
But neither player has to deal
With the loss of their son.

At the end of the game
The board is reset,
But at the end of a war
All your have is regret.

Children

Children die
In times of war,
It's happening now
Like it's happened before.

Some die of thirst
When we cut off their water,
And some bleed from bullets
Such unnecessary slaughter.

It doesn't seem fair
And it doesn't seem right
That children are bombed
While sleeping at night,

So if you care for the kids
Then please fight no more,
Because children die
In times of war.

Artists At War

You just write poems
When you could do more.
Are you not aware
We're a country at war?

It's a waste of time
To dance and sing,
Pick up a gun
And do something.

You like to paint
And you like to draw,
But if we lose this fight
Then what's it all for?

Well that's the thing
You don't understand,
We make all this art
Because war should be banned.

Pawns For The Rich

We're just pawns for the rich,
Our lives don't matter.
They just keep us around
To help their wallets get fatter.

We should die for our country
And do it with pride.
They say these wars are for justice
But the truth is they lied.

These wars only happen
Because they want more power.
Wars give them money
While our graves get a flower.

They don't care if you live,
They'll leave your body in a ditch.
Why can't you see
We're just pawns for the rich.

Remember

Remember those who fell before,
Lost their lives in pointless war,
Died believing in a noble cause,
But never got the chance to pause,
And question why they had to fight?
Why they had to die that night?
While the men who start the battle
Stand aside, treat them like cattle.

The soldiers who shot and killed each other
Had more in common with one another,
Than the bastards who gave the command
But never saw the horrors of no man's land.
All the money that's made in war
Is made through deaths of brave and poor,
Who never get to see the spoils
Instead they suffer through the toils.
And then we parade their memory,
Never truly understanding the treachery,
The countless horrors they endured
So that investments could be secured.

Remember those who have fallen,
But never forget why they died.
The greed of those in power
Is the reason their mothers cried.
Don't disrespect the soldiers.
They died for a noble lie.
But before the past repeats itself,
We must all ask ourselves…
Why?

Closing Thoughts

Thank you for making it to the end of this book. I hope there were parts of it that you enjoyed, and parts that made you think.

Despite all the problems I have discussed in this book, I haven't given up on humanity. Through my work at Karuna and with the Socialist Party, I see amazing, compassionate human beings every day, fighting hard to make a positive change, and they give me hope that things can get better.

It is not too late for us. The deadline grows ever closer but it has not yet been reached.

If you are interested in hearing more of what I have to say then you can find me on Instagram, my handle is very creatively @ryan_lyddall. Feel free to reach out to me and discuss your thoughts on the poems.

I also have a youtube channel, again creatively named Ryan Lyddall. It only contains a couple of videos of me speaking at socialist party meetings at the moment but I plan to use it more for some upcoming projects I have planned.

I have one final poem for you now, Poem for a Better Tomorrow, and it serves as a mirror to the poem I started the book with. I tried to make this one a bit less depressing.

Poem For a Better Tomorrow

The world in which we are raised
Is how we think the world must be.
But if we all come together
We can rebuild our society.

The change must start from within,
With unlearning what we think we know
Abolishing this wretched system
And deciding where we should go.

Stop doing what's best for profit
Start doing what's best for mankind
Let's realise human potential
And stop choosing to be blind

Humanity can survive
Without needless death and exploitation
We can make this planet better
For every future generation

Because there's more to us more than this
This system of brutality
Together we have the power
To make a better reality

We must focus on the holes
Shine a light on all the flaws
Even if this hard fought battle
Doesn't win us much applause

We march towards our demise
But it's not too late you see
We still have the potential
To save our society

It is never too late for a bad person to do good. The bad they have done is never forgotten and they may never be redeemed, but it is never too late for them to choose to start doing good.

In the same vein - it is never too late to change the world, it is never too late to save the world. The damage of the past is already done, but we can save what remains.

We must save what remains.

Printed in Great Britain
by Amazon